Warthog

by Grace Hansen

Abdo
AFRICAN ANIMALS
Kids

abdopublishing.com

Published by Abdo Kids, a division of ABDO, P.O. Box 398166, Minneapolis, Minnesota 55439.

Printed in the United States of America, North Mankato, Minnesota.

102017

012018

THIS BOOK CONTAINS RECYCLED MATERIALS

Photo Credits: iStock, Shutterstock

Production Contributors: Teddy Borth, Jennie Forsberg, Grace Hansen

Design Contributors: Dorothy Toth, Laura Mitchell

Publisher's Cataloging in Publication Data

Names: Hansen, Grace, author.

Title: Warthog / by Grace Hansen.

Description: Minneapolis, Minnesota : Abdo Kids, 2018. | Series: African animals |
Includes glossary, index and online resource (page 24).

Identifiers: LCCN 2017943139 | ISBN 9781532104220 (lib.bdg.) | ISBN 9781532105340 (ebook) |
ISBN 9781532105906 (Read-to-me ebook)

Subjects: LCSH: Warthog--Juvenile literature. | Zoology--Africa--Juvenile literature.

Classification: DDC 599.63 --dc23

LC record available at https://lccn.loc.gov/2017943139

Table of Contents

Warthog Habitat 4

Body 10

Food 16

Baby Warthogs 18

More Facts 22

Glossary 23

Index 24

Abdo Kids Code. 24

Warthog Habitat

Warthogs live in many parts of Africa. They are mostly found in **savannas**.

Warthogs spend most of their days rolling in water or mud. They do this to cool down.

At night, warthogs snuggle up in their dens. They do this to stay warm. They also do it to avoid nighttime **predators**.

Body

Warthogs have very little hair. But they do have **manes** on their backs.

Warthogs can grow to be 35 to 59 inches (89 to 150 cm) long. They weigh between 120 and 250 pounds (54.4 and 113.4 kg).

Adult warthogs have four sharp **tusks**. They use their tusks to protect themselves.

Food

Warthogs are **grazers**. They use their snouts to dig for roots. They also eat grasses and other plants.

Baby Warthogs

Female warthogs often have 2 to 4 babies. Some have up to 8 babies. Babies stay in dens until they are 7 weeks old.

Baby warthogs drink their mother's milk for 6 months. They start trying new foods, like plants, at 2 months old.

More Facts

- Warthogs are related to pigs.
- Warthogs look tough. But they would rather flee from danger than fight. They run to their dens and hide.
- Warthogs got their name for the warts (or large bumps) on their faces. Males have 4 bumps and females have 2.

Glossary

grazer – an animal that feeds on growing grass.

mane – the long hair on the back and sides of an animal's neck.

predator – an animal that hunts other animals for food.

savanna – a large area of grass with few trees.

tusk – a long, large, pointed tooth that sticks out from the mouth of some animals.

Index

Africa 4

babies 18, 20

body 10

den 8, 18

food 16, 20

habitat 4

mane 10

mud 6

predators 8

size 12

snout 16

tusk 14

water 6

weight 12